Royal Borough of Kingston Upon Thames

KT-548-229

ON THE TRAIL OF
THE

VICTORIANS
IN BRITAIN

PETER CHRISP

W

KINGSTON LIBRARIES
KT 0934378 4

FRANKLIN WATTS

First published in 1999 by Franklin Watts

Copyright © 1999 Franklin Watts

Franklin Watts
338 Euston Road
London NW1 3BH

Franklin Watts Australia
Level 17/207 Kent Street
Sydney, NSW 2000

All rights reserved.

A CIP record for this book is available from the British Library.

Dewey number: 941.081

ISBN: 978 0 7496 3588 6

Printed in Dubai

Franklin Watts is a division of Hachette Children's Books.

Planning and production by Discovery Books Ltd
Editor: Helena Attlee and Helen Lanz
Designer: Simon Borrough
Consultant: Tim Copeland
Art: Stuart Carter, Stefan Chabluk

Photographs: All photographs by Alex Ramsay except for: Beamish Museum: page 22 top; Patrick Ward/Corbis: page 12; Thomas Crane, from *About Town*: 13 right; The Mary Evans Picture Library: pages 4, 7, 9 right, 11 left, 12 top, 15 top, 25 both, 27 both; The National Coal Mining Museum, Wakefield: pages 8-9; The National Trust Photographic Library: pages 19 both (Andreas von Einsiedel); The Ragged School Museum: page 23; The Salvation Army International Heritage Centre: page 21 (bottom)

KINGSTON UPON THAMES Libraries	
0934378 4	
J942.08	PETERS
26-Oct-2009	£5.99
T D	

CONTENTS

WHO WERE THE VICTORIANS?

It is about a hundred years since Queen Victoria died, but many things happened during her long and great reign that still affect our lives today.

Queen Victoria with her husband, Prince Albert, and five of their nine children.

The Victorian Age was a time of enormous change. When the Queen came to the throne in 1837, most British people lived in the countryside. By the time she died in 1901, more than three quarters of them lived in large towns and cities. Britain's population had risen during this period from 16 to 37 million.

Many of the people living in large towns and cities had jobs in factories. Some of the vast buildings where they worked can still be seen today. Many of our schools, libraries, town halls, hospitals and museums are Victorian, too, and millions of us live in Victorian houses or flats.

The Forth Railway Bridge looked like nothing ever built before. This was the style of the future.

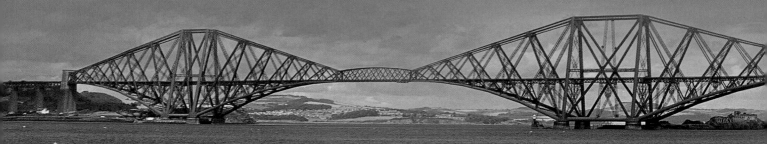

Manchester Town Hall, like many Victorian buildings, was built in a grand architectural style from the past.

Several of the things that we take for granted today, such as photography, telephones and cars, were invented during Queen Victoria's reign. There were new building materials too. The Forth railway bridge (below), was the first bridge in the world made from something called 'mild steel'. It was part of the new network of railways that connected Victorian Britain from end to end.

Many factory towns had grand town halls. Manchester Town Hall (above) was built in 1868. It is designed in a style called 'neo-gothic', based on the cathedrals and churches of the Middle Ages. The rich factory owners of such towns were proud of their cities, and wanted their town halls to look as grand as possible.

VICTORIAN FACTORIES

During Victoria's reign, Britain became the richest country in the world. It was nicknamed the 'workshop of the world'.

In cities like Bradford, Leeds and Manchester, the Victorians built huge factories powered by steam engines. Most of the world's iron, steel and cotton cloth was made in British factories.

This is Manningham Mills, a silk factory built in Bradford in 1873. When the chimney was built, Samuel Lister, the mill owner, climbed up and smashed a bottle of champagne against it, as if he were launching a ship. He named his chimney 'Lister's Pride'.

The height of Lister's chimney ensured that the smoke was carried high up into the sky, far above Bradford.

Lister's chimney is 76m high. Its enormous height is a sign that Lister was very proud of his factory and wanted everyone to know that it was there. There were more than 130 factories in Bradford alone, each belching out thick smoke. A stinking, yellow smog lay over the city, blocking out the sun, and damaging the health of all the people who had to breathe the polluted air.

Industrial areas in Victorian Britain.

Most Victorian factories have closed down now, but some have been made into museums. Leeds and Bradford each have an industrial museum. They are housed in buildings that were once wool mills. There you can see steam-powered machines in action. This will help you to imagine what it was like to work in a Victorian factory.

Factory workers spent between 70 and 90 hours each week at the machines, which were deafeningly noisy. The rooms were hot and dusty, and the air was hard to breathe. Until the 1830s, most textile factories employed children as young as six. They were a cheap source of labour.

Many Victorians were shocked by the lives of child workers in the factories. A series of laws was passed, limiting the use of child labour.

COAL MINES

Coal was the main source of power in Victorian times. It was used for cooking and heating, and for driving machinery, trains and steam ships.

▼ Most British coal mines have closed down now. The Caphouse Colliery in Wakefield has reopened as the National Coal Mining Museum.

Before Queen Victoria came to the throne, only about 9 million tonnes of coal was mined in Britain each year. By the end of her reign, coal production had risen to 198 million tonnes a year. Much of this coal was shipped abroad, and sold all over the world.

At the National Coal Mining Museum in Wakefield you can travel in a cage deep under the ground to see the narrow tunnels where the miners

spent their working lives. From 1790 until 1985, this was a working mine called the Caphouse Colliery. Today, it helps us to understand what a hard life Victorian miners must have led.

Being a miner has always been very dangerous. In December 1866, the Oaks Colliery in Barnsley blew up. The deaths of 361 men and boys were recorded. Between 1850 and 1914, mining accidents caused 1,000 deaths in Britain each year. Sometimes a tunnel flooded or its roof caved in, crushing the miners beneath it. Miners could be poisoned by underground gas. This gas could explode if ignited by a spark from a miner's pickaxe hitting a stone.

▲ Victorian miners knelt down to work, like this model in the National Coal Mining Museum. They hacked at the coal with pickaxes.

N

Victorian coal fields.

TRAPPERS
Until the 1840s, children as young as five worked down mines as trappers. For 12 hours a day, they sat in the dark, opening trap doors to allow the coal carts through. The trap doors were kept closed to stop gas spreading throughout the mine. Several explosions were caused by trappers who fell asleep or wandered off to play, leaving their trap doors open.

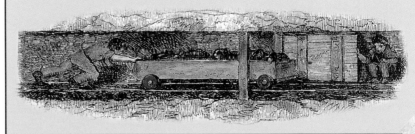

THE RAILWAYS

During the Victorian era, hundreds of miles of railway lines were laid across Britain.

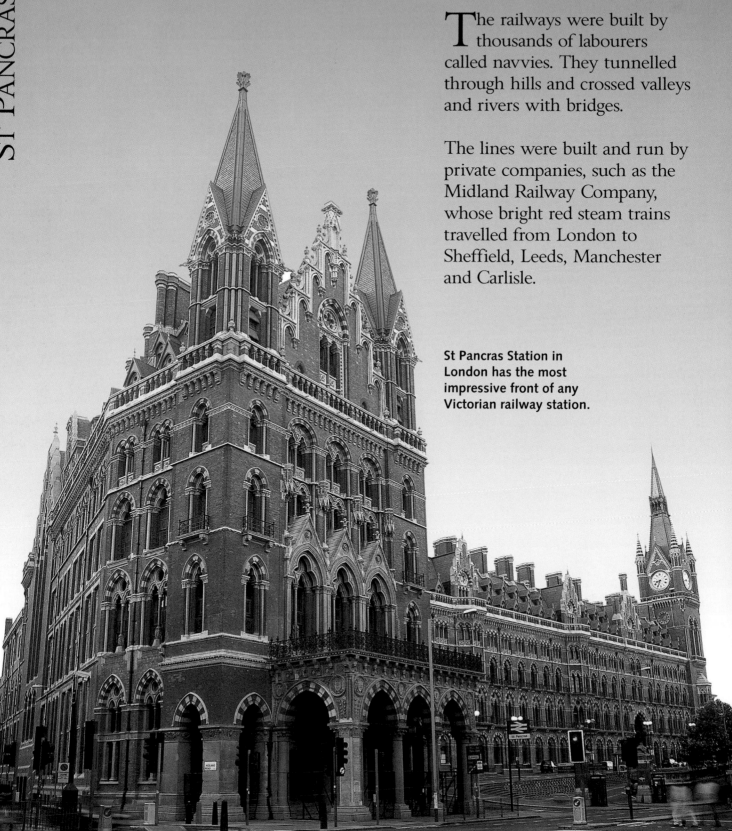

The railways were built by thousands of labourers called navvies. They tunnelled through hills and crossed valleys and rivers with bridges.

The lines were built and run by private companies, such as the Midland Railway Company, whose bright red steam trains travelled from London to Sheffield, Leeds, Manchester and Carlisle.

St Pancras Station in London has the most impressive front of any Victorian railway station.

The Midlands' main London station was St Pancras, which was built between 1863 and 1874 and still stands today. At the front there is a huge red brick building, decorated with towers and spires, rather like a cathedral. This was a hotel called the Midland Grand, where rich visitors to London could stay in comfort. The grandeur of the building reflects the importance of railway travel in Victorian times.

Behind the station's brick front, there is the train shed, to shelter trains and passengers from the rain. Its roof had to be as high as possible, because of all the smoke from the steam engines.

The station's Midland Grand Hotel stood empty for many years after it was closed in 1935. It still had a wonderful interior, despite the peeling wallpaper.

The engineers built this enormous roof at St Pancras out of iron. It was 30m high and 73m wide. This was the biggest roof in the world without inside supports, such as columns. People were amazed when they first saw it. What was holding it up?

The railways changed people's lives. For the first time, ordinary people could see for themselves what other parts of Britain looked like. Thousands of city workers travelled on outings to the seaside and countryside. Rail travel also changed people's working lives. It meant that they could work a long way from their homes.

Victorian engineers designed bridges and tunnels. Teams of thousands of men worked to move the earth, using only pickaxes, shovels and other hand tools.

THE SEASIDE

The new railways allowed people who lived in cities to travel to the seaside for the first time. Many seaside resorts in Britain still have fine Victorian buildings along the sea front.

Victoria Pier, South Shore.   Blackpool.

WINTER GARDENS

People from all classes enjoyed a trip to the seaside. The working classes went there on day trips from the factory towns. Richer people went for a week in the summer, staying in hotels or guest houses.

These are two of Blackpool's piers. The Central Pier (below) was built between 1867 and 1868. The Victorian postcard (left) shows the South Pier, built in 1893.

Every seaside town wanted visitors who would spend money, and one way to attract them was to build a pier. Blackpool was not happy with just one pier. The town built three, and they still attract visitors today.

This wooden pier was built at Swanage in 1893.

PUNCH AND JUDY

One popular seaside entertainment was a Punch and Judy puppet show. Children loved watching the bad behaviour of the wicked Mr Punch. You can still see Punch and Judy in some seaside towns today.

❦ PUNCH · AND · JUDY ❦

HAVE you a penny? well then, stay!
Haven't you any? don't go away!
Punch holds receptions all through the day,
Squeaking aloud to gather a crowd,
Scolding at Toby, beating his Wife,
Frightening the Constable out of his life,
And making jokes in a terrible passion,
As is Mr. Punch's peculiar fashion;
For this is his old, delightful plan
Of getting as many pence as he can.
   Then away he'll jog,
   With his Wife and his Dog,
   New folks to meet
   In the very next street.

The showman beats a drum to draw a crowd for Mr Punch.

The first piers were just wooden platforms with a few shelters and refreshment stalls. People enjoyed strolling along the deck, breathing in the fresh sea air and looking down at the waves below.

As more piers were built, new attractions were added to them. They were given shops and pavilions where bands played.

Not all towns could afford piers like Blackpool's. Swanage in Dorset had a much simpler pier. Although there were no amusements or bandstands, people could go on boat trips from the pier's end.

The number of piers built in the Victorian age reflects the growing wealth of the seaside towns. This was because of the visitors brought by the new railway lines.

HOMES FOR THE WORKERS

Industrial cities like Leeds, Manchester and Sheffield grew very quickly. The workers lived close to their work, often in badly-built houses.

These workers' houses in Leeds are called 'back-to-backs'. To save space, each building was made up of two houses, joined by a shared back wall. By 1886, Leeds had 49,000 houses like this. Other industrial cities grew at a similar speed. Many back-to-backs are still lived in today. They have been modernised to make them more comfortable.

A single house in a back-to-back might have only two rooms. There was only one bedroom upstairs. Written evidence tells us that many families slept in a shared bed. The downstairs room was used for everything else: cooking, eating, washing and as an extra sleeping area. In these crowded conditions, illness spread very quickly.

These back-to-backs have been modernised, with inside toilets, running water and extra rooms in the roofs.

14

This Victorian photograph shows back-to-backs in Staithes, Yorkshire. The woman has to carry all the water she needs in a pair of buckets.

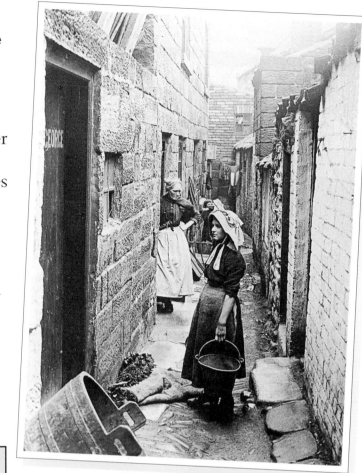

Families used a toilet in the street, which they shared with their neighbours. They collected their water from an outside tap. The water was often dirty and spread terrible diseases like cholera and typhoid. Between 1848 and 1849, 62,000 people died from cholera.

From the 1850s, the government tried to make cities healthier places to live. They improved water supplies and built new sewers. In many places, we still use Victorian water pipes and sewers.

SALTAIRE
Not all workers' houses were badly built. The Bradford mill owner, Titus Salt, moved his factories and workers to the countryside where he built a new town that he called Saltaire. Each house had gas lighting, running water and an outside toilet.

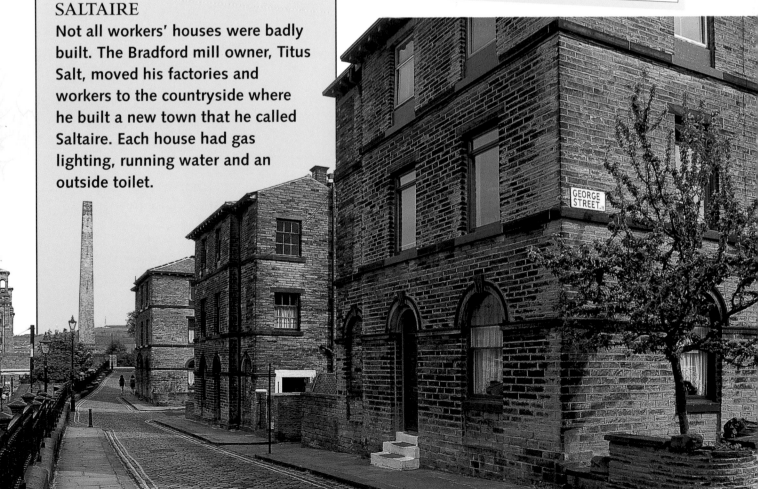

MIDDLE-CLASS HOMES

While the working classes lived close to the factories where they worked, middle-class people preferred to live in the suburbs, away from city centres.

Houses like this one were built all around the outskirts of London.

These are middle-class Victorian houses in Putney, a suburb in south-west London. There are Victorian suburbs similar to this all over Britain. Every morning, from Monday to Saturday, the men who lived here travelled on a train or a horse-drawn bus to the city, where they worked in offices.

Suburban homes were richly decorated, with patterned wallpaper and carpets. The walls were covered with pictures and there were usually ornaments everywhere.

Every middle-class family employed a servant to do the housework. Many of them also had a cook and one or two housemaids.

Some of the reasons for living in the suburbs are the same today as they were in Victorian England. The air was much cleaner there than it was in the smoky city and the streets were quiet. After a day working among the crowds and noise, Victorian men wanted to escape to the peace of their suburban houses. They also looked down on the poor as their 'inferiors', and they did not want to live near them.

The servants heated the water and cooked the meals on a coal-fired kitchen range.

A typical middle-class home was semi-detached – two houses joined by a shared side wall.

HOMES FOR THE RICH

In many parts of British countryside, you can visit large stately homes, where rich Victorian landowners once lived.

▲ From outside, Lanhydrock looks like a seventeenth-century house, but its interior is all Victorian.

▼ On Sundays, the Robartes family and their servants went to the local church, St Helier, which stands next to the house.

One of the best houses to visit is Lanhydrock in Cornwall. It was the home of Baron Robartes of Truro, whose vast wealth came from farms and tin mines on his Cornish lands. His family had lived here since the 1600s, but their house was badly damaged by fire in 1881. The baron immediately set about rebuilding Lanhydrock and it has hardly changed since. Visiting this house is like travelling back in time to the 1880s.

▲ This is Lady Robartes' morning room, where she drank tea with her friends.

▲ Victorian houses open to the public.

At the time the new house was built, there were thousands of large families sharing one or two rooms in Britain's industrial cities, yet at Lanhydrock there were many rooms, each built with a special purpose in mind. The names of the different rooms in grand, Victorian houses tell us something about the way that rich people spent their time. The morning room was used by Lady Robartes to receive her visitors; the men went to the smoking room to enjoy their cigars after dinner, and they played billiards in the billiard room. The baron called his house a 'simple family home'. To anyone else, it would be a palace!

SERVANTS

Dozens of servants were needed to run houses of this size. There were footmen, to answer the front door, housemaids to light the coal fires and clean the rooms, and laundry maids to wash the clothes and bed linen. Some of the rich wouldn't even get dressed in the morning without servants to help them.

The maid who served Lady Robartes' tea slept in this little room in the attic.

RELIGION

The Victorians built thousands of churches and chapels all over Britain. Many of them are still standing and serve to remind us how important religion was in the Victorian Age.

For almost everyone, religion meant Christianity. Sunday was called the 'Lord's day', when millions of Christians went to a church or a chapel to worship God.

Some Victorian churches are still used. Others have been converted into houses, shops or flats and some stand empty like the St Vincent's Street Church in Glasgow. This church was designed to look like a Greek temple.

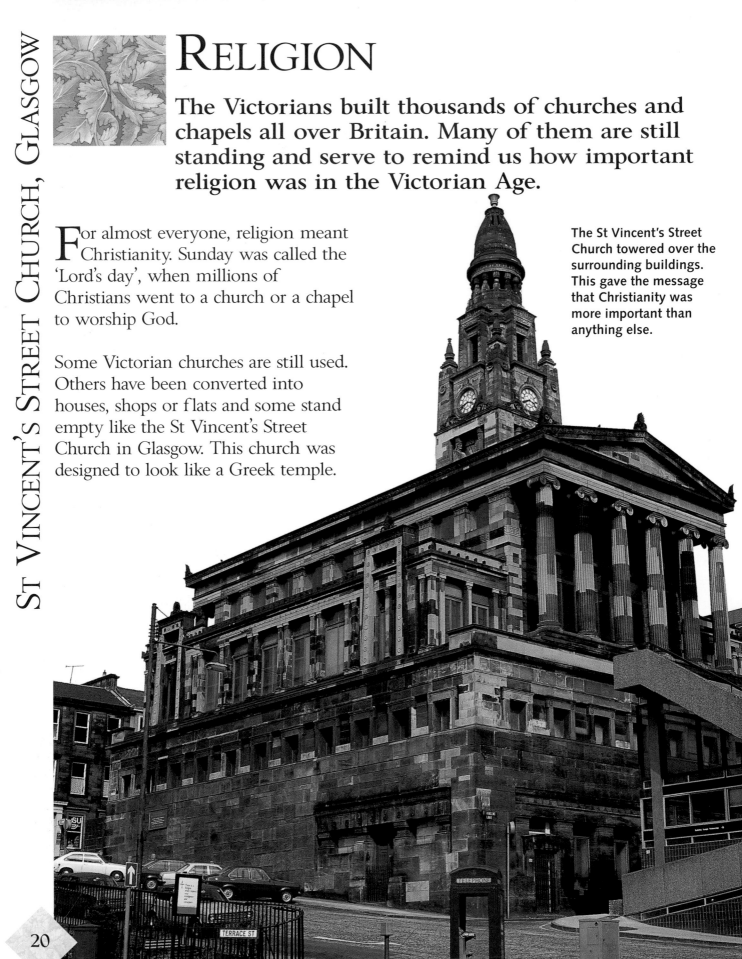

The St Vincent's Street Church towered over the surrounding buildings. This gave the message that Christianity was more important than anything else.

▼ Tombs of rich Victorian merchants and their families in Glasgow.

Glasgow has a big cemetery on a hill, rising above the city, where the rich were buried. It is called the Necropolis, which means 'city of the dead', and it is covered with statues and grand tombs.

Cemeteries like this are wonderful places to gather information about the lives of the Victorians. If you read the writing on Victorian tomb stones, you will find that large families were common, and many children died young. The large number of child deaths was caused by infectious diseases for which no cure was known at that time.

THE SALVATION ARMY

Poor people in the big cities had less time for religion. Many preferred to go to a pub rather than a church on a Sunday. In 1878, William Booth founded the Salvation Army to bring Christianity to the city poor. His followers wore uniforms, like soldiers. They marched through the slums, playing music and preaching on street corners and in pubs.

The Salvation Army, as in this picture, still marches through the streets of many British cities on Sundays.

SCHOOLS

Today, every child in Britain has the right to a free education. Many poor Victorian children never went to school. As soon as they were old enough, they worked for a living.

Many of the schools built by the Victorians are still standing today. Some of them still have the separate entrances for boys and girls clearly marked.

The picture below shows Bonner Street Board School in Hackney, built in 1875. It was one of hundreds of new schools built in the 1870s for poor children. The schools were paid for by local taxes called rates. They were called 'board schools' because the ratepayers elected a 'board' of people to set up and run them. Like many Victorian schools, Bonner Street is still used as a school today.

◀ Boys and girls were educated separately. You can often still see the signs above the doors to show the separate entrances.

▼ The Bonner Street Board School is still in use as a primary school today.

Before the Board schools were built, the only places for the poorest children to go were free 'ragged schools', run by private charities. Many of these children worked in the factories each morning before school. They went back to work after school until 10 o'clock at night.

Bonner Street school has three floors. Each floor was a separate school. The ground floor was the Infants' School for boys and girls, the next floor was for boys aged between seven and 13. Girls of this age had their school on the top floor.

▲ In the countryside, the Victorians built much smaller schools, like this one at Knighton in Wales.

▲ This picture shows the Ragged School in East London which was made into a museum. Here you can sit in a Victorian classroom and find out what a lesson was like.

23

THE POOR

Victorian Britain was the richest country in the world. Yet life could be terribly hard for the poor.

There was only one place where the poor could go for help, the workhouse. Those unable to look after themselves included the old, the sick, the orphaned and abandoned children.

There were workhouses all over Britain. The huge building below is the Andover Workhouse in Hampshire. It was called a workhouse because the poor people who stayed here had to work for their bed and food. At Andover, they smashed up old animal bones to make fertiliser for farmers.

The men sit in strict rows to eat their meal at the Marylebone Workhouse, London, in 1900.

Like board schools, workhouses were paid for by local taxes called rates. The ratepayers worried that their money might be spent looking after people who could find work, but were too lazy to do so. To discourage the 'undeserving poor', a workhouse was designed to be an unpleasant place to live. People only went there when they had nowhere else to go.

Some of the early workhouses were badly run. To save money, the poor people were given hardly any food. At Andover in 1845, the inmates were so hungry that they gnawed at the bones they were supposed to be breaking up.

Under the rules of the workhouse, men, women, boys and girls all lived separately. Everyone had to wear a uniform. Conditions gradually improved and some workhouses even organised outings for children.

◄ Every poor person was terrified of losing their freedom and ending up in a workhouse.

▲ This picture shows the Women's quarters of the Lambeth Workhouse in London.

CRIME AND PUNISHMENT

Before the Victorian Age, men, women and children were locked up together in overcrowded prisons.

The Victorians invented a new type of prison, designed to stop criminals mixing with each other. Prisoners were kept away from each other and locked up in small cells. This was called the separate system. The Victorians thought that, kept away from the bad influence of the others, some prisoners might learn to live better lives.

The great gateway to Wormwood Scrubs is like the entrance to a castle.

The prisoners spent almost all their time alone in their cells. The only time that they went outside was when they were taken into a yard to walk for exercise.

Wormwood Scrubs prison was built between 1874 and 1890, by the prisoners themselves. The first block was built by only nine prisoners who lived in a temporary shack. This allowed 50 more prisoners to move in and build another block, and so on.

When they were exercising, the prisoners had to wear masks to stop them recognising each other.

Church was an important part of prison life in Victorian times. The picture below shows the chapel at Pentonville, where the men were taken on Sundays. You can see that each prisoner is in a separate box, to stop him seeing any other prisoner. The warders look down from above to make sure that no-one is talking.

Prisoners caught speaking were punished. One punishment was 'turning the crank'. This was a handle which turned a drum full of sand. The prisoner had to turn this thousands of times before he was allowed to eat or sleep. Turning the crank was meant to be pointless. This made it more of a punishment.

We still keep thousands of prisoners in prisons built by the Victorians. However, the crank and the separate system are no longer in use.

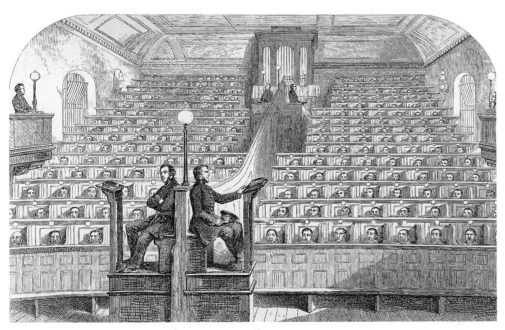

The pews in the prison chapel were divided to prevent the prisoners from seeing each other.

THE VICTORIANS AND US

Following the trail of the Victorians is never difficult - there are signs of the Victorian era all around us in Britain today.

Many museums have reconstructions of Victorian rooms.

Look out for Victorian statues. This one is of the explorer, David Livingstone.

Look around where you live. Your nearest town may be full of Victorian houses, churches and chapels. Your local hospital may be Victorian, and so may your school. Important places like town halls and libraries are often housed in grand, Victorian buildings. They will often have the date that they were finished carved on the front. Look for a date between 1837 and 1901. This is the easiest way to spot a Victorian building.

The Victorians built many museums, too, such as London's Natural History Museum, which houses a collection of plants, insects, bones and stuffed animals.

Many buildings, such as London's Natural History Museum, are built in the 'gothic' style.

Your local museum, or even somebody in your family may have some Victorian photographs. The camera was invented during Victoria's reign and it became extremely fashionable to have photographic portraits taken of every member of the family. Looking at these pictures will help you along the trail of finding out about the Victorians.

The next time you travel on a train, think of the thousands of Victorian workers who laid the lines and built the bridges and tunnels.

The Victorian period ended on 22 January, 1901, when Queen Victoria died at the age of 81. She had reigned for 63 years. This was the longest reign in British history. During the Victorian Age Britain became richer and more powerful than ever before.

GLOSSARY

back-to-back
a pair of cheaply-built houses joined by a shared back wall to save space

board school
a Victorian school for children aged between three and thirteen. Board schools were mostly built in the 1870s and 1880s, especially in the centre of large towns and cities

cholera
a very serious infectious disease

colliery
a coal mine

engineer
someone trained to design bridges, railways, roads and tunnels

Gothic
a style of architecture common in the Middle Ages. The Victorians copied the Gothic style, designing buildings with pointed arches and steep, high roofs

mill
a building fitted with machines used to grind materials

pier
a structure running out over the sea, built for pleasure and leisure

separate system
a method of running a prison in which the prisoners were not allowed to have any contact with each other

suburb
the outlying areas of towns, where the middle classes lived

trappers
children who worked down mines opening and closing trap doors to let coal carts through. The doors were kept closed to stop gas spreading

typhoid
a very dangerous, infectious disease, often caught by drinking dirty water

workhouse
a building which provided food and shelter to the poorest people, who were expected to work (unless they were too sick). In Scotland, they were called 'poorhouses'

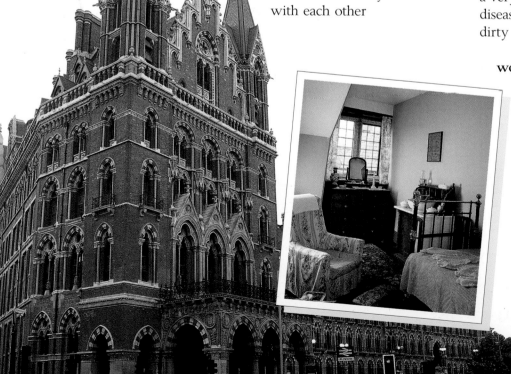

TIMELINE

1837   Queen Victoria crowned at the age of 18

1839-
1840   First photographs taken, by Louis Daguerre in France and William Henry Fox-Talbot in Britain

1840   Postage stamps introduced

1842   The Mines Act bans employment of boys under ten and all women and girls underground in the coal mines

1844   The Factory Act limits the working day for children under 13 to six and a half hours

1844-
1845   8,000km of railway track built across Britain

1851   London is now Britain's largest city, with 2.4 million people

1854-
1856   The Crimean War fought by Britain and France against Russia

1861   The death of Queen Victoria's husband, Prince Albert

1862   Blackpool's first pier built

1870   The Education Act sets up boards to provide 'elementary' education for children aged five to ten

1873   Manningham Mills built in Bradford

1880   All British children have to go to school until the age of ten

1881   London's Natural History Museum opens

1886   The steel Forth Railway Bridge built

1891   Elementary schooling made free

1901   Death of Queen Victoria

PLACES TO VISIT

Angus Folk Museum, Glamis, Forfar, Tayside, Scotland DD8 1RT: A museum of nineteenth-century life in Scotland.

The Bluebell Railway, Sheffield Park, near Uckfield, East Sussex: Travel on a real steam train on this line, which runs between Horsted Keynes and Sheffield Park. Discover the smells, sights and sounds of steam engines!

Bradford Industrial Museum, Eccleshill, Bradford, Yorkshire BD2 3HP: A wool mill converted into a museum of factory life.

Great Britain, Bristol docks, Bristol: A famous Victorian steamship.

Lanhydrock, Bodmin, Cornwall, PL30 5AD: A grand stately home of the 1880s.

Inverary Jail, Church Square, Inverary, Argyll, Scotland, PA32 8TX: A museum of nineteenth-century prison life, with people dressed as warders and prisoners. Try out a cell for yourself, and have a go at 'turning the crank'.

North of England Open Air Museum, Beamish, County Durham DH9 0RG: Open air museum with a street of Victorian buildings.

Ragged School Museum, Copperfield Rd, London E3 4RR: Museum showing the lives of poor children in London. Offers Victorian role-play lessons for groups of children.

Welsh Folk Museum, St Fagans, Cardiff, CF5 6XB: A museum of buildings including a Victorian school, a chapel and a terrace of ironworkers' houses.

INDEX